Clement Akuo-Ehohnzi was born in a typical Bakossi village in Southern Cameroon. He spent his childhood in this unique setting where he observed the wispy remnants of a culture once colorful and alive, and vowed internally to give new life to it. Akuo-Ehohnzi currently lives in Maryland developing his craft. He studied mass communication and journalism, is a fellow of the MacDowell Peterborough New Hampshire, and the author of *The Villain Within*.

Before my curiosity was aroused in the scanty literature of the Ngoe Dynasty, that intrigue was ignited by my father John Akuo-Ehohnzi's account when I was a kid. I have not read or heard a more captivating version than his. As a catechist, he was compelled to relinquish his traditional powers and beliefs like his following brothers, Chief Dominic Edi, Emmanuel Ntube, Thomas Ekahkpe, Peter Nsong, Lawrence Esambe, Soh Ehabe, Athanasius Nzikuoh, and Raphael Nzikang, all from the Ngeme-Ngoe pedigree embracing the Catholic faith. These people, in various ways, instilled a sense of awakening in me.

Clement Akuo-Ehohnzi

PILGRIMAGE INTO THE WOMB OF A BANTU DYNASTY

AUSTIN MACAULEY PUBLISHERS™

LONDON • CAMBRIDGE • NEW YORK • SHARJAH

Ordering Information
Quantity sales: Special discounts are available on quantity purchases by corporations, associations, and others. For details, contact the publisher at the address below.

Publisher's Cataloging-in-Publication data
Akuo-Ehohnzi, Clement
Pilgrimage into the Womb of a Bantu Dynasty

ISBN 9781638290001 (Paperback)
ISBN 9781638290018 (ePub e-book)

Library of Congress Control Number: 2022921332

www.austinmacauley.com/us

First Published 2023
Austin Macauley Publishers LLC
40 Wall Street, 33rd Floor, Suite 3302
New York, NY 10005
USA

mail-usa@austinmacauley.com
+1 (646) 512576

Even though the quest to understand the African belief systems has alienated me from religion as postulated and practiced by Christians and Muslims, I nevertheless listen to some of their preachers. According to Dr. Mike Murdock, one doesn't need many people to make it. You need only one person who recognizes and believes in your vision and dreams, and the rest will be history. That's precisely what happened to me when I strolled like a lamb in search of a bearing and stumbled on this Tanzanian-born illustrious son, Mr. Mohamed Matope. It's hard to quantify his level of selflessness. Creative ability is a personal journey. However, it can never be smooth and accomplished without the people one deals with daily. This is why I'm indebted to the quality One Care Team of nurses and staff, especially Regness Mbuya, Deshola Adebayo and Amon Chafukira. My brothers and friends, Bishop Lawrence Kang, Philip Timbu, and Musa Yumouh for their continued support. Three very special women, Esther Muabe, Marie Akonjang, and the one and only Gladys Malike for their endless support. Fatherly love to my son Collins Nzikang and daughter Lydien Parsa for being patient with me through the years of my absence.

When it journeys through three wombs
The Bantu pedigrees believe and agree
The lifecycle of an individual is complete.
Nevertheless, death determinant factor in,
The procedural selection for the completion,
Igniting the debate for reincarnation.
And rooting the life after death contention.
From creed to creed, race to race
Variation in traditions and cultures
And the conflicts in denominational beliefs,
All account for the admissible disagreements.

Going by conceptual and physical observations,
The human span undergoes three distinctive natural
seasons.
The primary follows a natal yet mysterious course,
Of conception and the unfolding into a woman's womb.
That leads to the penultimate birth.
The complexity of sequences in human growth
The tumultuous chains of events before death
And internment into the earth,
From which the human body allegedly emanates,
After two mated cells to a zygote
Of living beings, are religiously formed and made

The Ngoe Dynasty of the Bantu people
Is rooted in the cognomen
Muane-Ngoh, meaning a cub of a feline
Juxtapositioned as a child born of a tiger or lion
After an encounter with Sang Diob Egum:
The Almighty God in the attributes of a feline
So extraordinary, capable of every physical move,
Jump, run, creep, scale with unbearable swiftness
The lion looking beyond the intrinsic
On a volcanic mountain, so dynamic
Named the Muane-Ngum Mountain,
Meaning the mountain of power
Now dormant and called Muanengumba.
Hence, the bedrock of many
Bantu ethnic and tribal patrimony.

The custodian of the Muane-Ngoe identity
Or better still, the children of Ngoe's identity
After centuries of movements and tribal hegemony
The results of patriarchal land rivalry
Remained a tribe and language known
From the colonial appellation,
As Bakossi and Akoose
Both denoting an epithet of dislike.
The tribe and language invoking hate imagery.
The colonial masters' mistreatment of her ancestry
Alienating the people from their history, geography
And the fervent spiritual alignment,
Of the divine direction of the Ngoe descent.
Blotting away Muane-Ngoe as the tribe,
Ngoe as the language of these people

And the lion or tiger as their symbol.

The Bantu lexicon interchangeably,
Employs the word soul and spirit to convey
The non-corporeal nature of human beings.
Nevertheless, the soul and the spirit are distinct
In meaning, applicable in usage and context.
The core of human life and serving as a link,
Between the human body and the spirit is the soul.
The spirit dwells within the celestial.
Having a direct and overriding role in the soul.
When alive, the soul remains a dominant matter.
While the spirit is an outer recessive matter
Assisting and guarding the soul during sleep
Makes possibility for humans to dream
Get revelations, even travel to strange places,
And get mysteriously cured of illnesses.
When death, the soul reunites with the spirit
After a scrutinized process to be able
To make encounters with humans possible.
Just as circumstances make them impossible.

Thereafter an individual is dead and buried
A third-grade constituent, the soul, leaves behind
The rejected remains of the bodily composition
And begins the journey to the spiritual womb.
The soul is subjected to sacred scrutiny.
Before its admittance into the heavenly
Body, because of the childhood purity
That every individual is born of
Is smeared by the corrupt nature of

The human species already in existence.
This contaminates and degrades the soul;
To the stage of impurity, inviting the need,
For a cathectic cosmic purge, have it upgraded,
To an elevated standard of purity
Acceptable into the promised immortal kingdom
That embodies the spiritual womb,
Known to be the cradle of mankind.

The very nature of human life
Interplayed with the advancement in science
And influenced by the arts and religious practices,
Have seemingly enhanced the awareness
Of the womb's first two journeys.
Even so, clouded and still shrouded, surprisingly,
In a mystery, is the womb's last journey
The sovereignty of the key to the verity
As of now, the creator keeps, sacredly.

Nothing has challenged the human ability
like understanding the mystery of the journey
Owing to the soul's inability to return to a decayed,
Cremated or an embalmed decomposed body.
Therefore, whatever the soul's partaking experience,
After death, it remains unknown and unfathomable.
The wisest philosophers have theorized.
Prophets and seers have exalted their whims.
Acclaimed representatives of God have dreamed
Yet, the mystery remains unlocked
Even Lazarus, whom Jesus wakes from dead
After weeping for the loss of a dedicated

Friend, and the challenge he faced
To convince his followers no power,
Was more than that of his father,
Had nothing extraordinary to say
To the jubilant and mesmerized crowd
About one of the greatest wonders performed,
In human history and religious records.
Perhaps, arguably Lazarus' soul still rested
Within the human breadth
And hovering in the milieu of his birth.
In the darkness of the earth
And hadn't transcended to the realm,
Of the underworld to undergo the experience
Of confronting spiritual scrutiny
To gain knowledge and mystery,
Of the after-death obscurity,
To report thereafter being resurrected,
The experience of life during that interlude.

The coercive forces of the universe,
Perhaps, and the power of the almighty
Makes no allowance for humanity
To retain absolute comprehension
Of the life after death
Just as it's mysterious before birth
To have an absolute understanding of conception
Even with the advancement in scientific innovation.
So it's with anyone who may wish to return,
To the earth after death to comprehend.

Arguably why Jesus Christ's body,
So to say, had to be flown away
In spirits, in agreement with the prophecy
And in concordance with the promise
He annunciated to his followers and disciples
To give credence to his apparition
In flesh and blood, days after his crucifixion.
Not even his apostles understood the mystery,
Of his eventual specter and ascendancy.

The resurrection and eventual ascendancy
Of Jesus Christ and seated with the Almighty
As postulated by Christians and Biblically
Centuries passed have not given way.
For any known group of persons or personality
To lay claim to this divine and sacred deed.
Except for the fallacious claim made
By a group of Bantu tribe, the Bayang people
Living within the Mbo-Bayang sanctuary
Of the tropical forest of Southern Cameroon
In their myth known in local parlance
As 'die-wake up,' has at best become debatable.
The claim that dead people
Of a certain Bayang clan within the tribe
Possess the ability after death
To hibernate, not in their place of birth.
Or in their area and city of growth
And live a secluded life,
Should they so desire,
Following their tradition
Having been initiated from conception.

This lingering centuries affirmation
With hardly any empirical verification
Has neither anthropological nor religious authentication.
But an alleged cultural trait still a myth in the minds,
Yet to be investigated empirically.
Or found to be credible with physical evidence,
By anyone else except the propagators.
Perhaps a conspiracy from religious practitioners,
And the influence of foreign values,
Have been the catalyst
To undermining this cultural trait
Inherent in this Bantu group of people,
And have constituted the impediment,
To understand the anthropological credulity of the myth.

Howbeit, every human born of a woman
Has a craving for a motherly bond.
The hankering doesn't start at birth,
The labor room and maternity ward
Or at infancy, but rather established
Right at the womb, many months and
Days before the push of the first cry,
When the search for comfortability
And survival becomes paramount for the baby
To endure the unwanted vestigial and defects
That stand in the way of the gamut of stages
The baby undergoes to stay alive.

The holistic essence of procreation
Be they physically normal children,
Mentally challenged or disability of any sort.

The womb remains the milieu of formation.
A distinctive habitat whose need for protection
And the dependable domain remains a sine qua non.
From father-mother bonding
To mother's shaped standards, including
That which she accepts and spurns
Growth enablers during conception.

The Bantu understanding of natality
Always made available precautionary
Herbs and enema to eliminate and destroy
Unwanted parasites and genetics borne diseases
To prevent birth difficulties and deformities,
That could eventually culminate in loss of lives.
The mastery to explore an unborn metaphysically,
And work to influence the baby iconography,
In strength, ability, and resilience
Form the basis of the Bantu cultural premise
That the character of the baby before birth
Readily translates into being on earth.
The absence of desirable and required care
From infancy is the greatest nightmare,
Infectious to any infant, toddler, and teenager.
The purposeful or not purposeful denial of
The child's sacrosanct right from the benefactor
Through disease, unprovoked and unanticipated misfortune
Often subsequently lead to premature death.
At best, derail and sidetrack the growth,
Process impacting the child's entire life.
These agonizing stories of miseries
Are disruptive of a plethora of infant potentials

Both at the embryonic and budding levels.

Ipso Facto, the absence of a mother at birth
Naturally, evoke questions of a child's being
Such as the causal effects of her death
The distinctive characteristics while on earth
Functional esthetic behavior and Interpersonal
relationships.
How serviceable were her deeds
Before the Almighty and ancestors
And how impacting was her community role
These questions could be rhetorical.
In other dimensions, absolutely nonsensical,
Whatever the case, they are all meant to recall
The memories and absence of a missing one
A child would live not knowing much about
To soothe the curiosity of a yearning heart.

The quest to understand the universal harmony
Structural, seasonal, and organizational precision
Investigating the normalization of natural pattern
Only one source could be at the origin.
The causes and effects, something
At the center through which everything
Was formed, made, created, and established
Sang Diob-Egum: The Almighty God.
The inquisitiveness to unfold what happens
Of a lost soul when naturality is understood,
Instilled a conscious awakening in mind,
Of an introspectively determined lad
To trace the whereabouts of his departed

Mother, whom fate denied the opportunity
To see and bond with, because, his birth,
Allegedly, hastened and caused her death.
Even more questionable, the untimely death
Of the woman who nursed him at birth.
These universal and puzzling anecdotes
And the quest for satisfactory answers
Let to mysterious encounters
That makes up the following gruesome
And poignant experience
Pregnant with normative antecedence
And summed up in both physical participation,
As well as spiritual guidance and observation.

The seventh of the eighth month
A male child took the first hazardous breath,
Of this partial and corrupted earth.
Haunted by his ancestral path
The last of three siblings none had survived
The gruesome circumstances of the denigrated
Household and precinct of their birth.
Besides, the small for date cane birth bed,
His mother, Mesode, lay helplessly,
Grasping for her breath, agonizingly.
Unanticipated breech-birth triggered encrustation,
Bleeding, causing unbearable pain and affliction.
The immutable unforeseen condition
Came with the dreadful and final call.

Mesode, by her appellation, meant tears.
Wipe away tears from a family

Subjected to the trauma of child lost,
A household figure or calamitous event
Whose occurrence destabilizes the family fabric.
This time, however, with her unexpected journey,
To the world beyond, she wasn't wiping away,
Tears, but surrendering her motherly responsibility.
Hence, giving the newborn a sobriquet;
Ejuape, translation, abandoned.

A thunderclap accompanied Mesode's farewell.
An instant torrential storm, cast a spell.
Leaving many homes roofless,
Wrecked farms and made corpses of crops.
The ancestors discountenance mourners admitted
Prevented the thatched hut that accommodated
Ejuape from crumbling as many had kissed the mud.
Was his birth solicited, and predestined,
Alternatively, a factor of chance?
Coming from a woman considered an embodiment of vice.
Allegations of sorcery linked to her name
Attaining an unforgivable degree
Eventually leading to child desertion.
The litany of contemptuous remarks
As the child contentiously wail,
Even among the wassail,
The number of somber and depressed hearts
Beaten by the trauma and willing to lend support
Increased as the news of the tragedy permeated.

Nursing baby Ejuape was a task
Relatives and well-wishers won't risk

To undertake at babyhood.
Born preterm, apprehensions of surviving probabilities
Preponderantly cast, proposals of being dumped
Wishing he passed on with her vile mother.
Villagers had seemingly abandoned Mesode
Long before death came calling
For having a not accommodating personality,
Exhibiting grossly inhumane and intolerable acts.
Wrapped in the torn garment, not that which the departed
Had set aside the thought of being infectious
Prohibited the lingering of her memories
Some sorcery jinx was linked to her belongings.

A distant relative of Mesode, Ma'Ahone,
Fifty-five could have been her age.
Vivacious and alluring in appearance
Though still keeping a melancholy mood
Reminiscing of her twenty years old
A mysterious ailment did claim
Grabbed the lifetime opportunity
To save a desperate and helpless baby.
And put significance into her pathetic life,
Of childlessness and solitude.

The challenge was a tall order to assume
A responsibility worth the risk to embrace
Frail, tender as a fresh cocoyam bud, and delicate
She mustered the guts and summoned her descent,
Intercession for a miraculous existence.
Ahone, meaning royal daughter, in other words
Daughter born of royal possessions.

So distinctive, openminded, and full of meekness.
If royalty was an epithet linked to her name
Her attributes as a woman of kindness were.
Full of will and energy with little proficiency
In her disposition to tackle the lifesaving responsibility
She employed her nursing ability,
As far as her skills could extend
An adroit mother and one who had nourished
Not only his lost son but other children
Soliciting for advice in every corner,
And engaged the services of the traditional healer.
Elumpeh, connotatively meaning, sent again.
By the ancestors as a sign of victory
Over a mishap and gladden the spirit,
Of parents whose households had experienced
Misery due to the loss of their firstborn
Or perhaps a household fate had denied,
It's matrimony, the tender cries of a baby,
After years of battling childlessness.
Denotatively, he responded to his name adequately.
The eyes and ears of the ancestors
Sent by the spirits as a community server
A traditional prophetic healer
Composed, foresighted, and lively with a proficient
The knack for healing and treating the scariest
Of cases, such as the staring challenge
That gave villagers no glimpse of hope.
Although, the premonition of the pending mishap
Ancestors had allegedly been confined to the people.

Elumpeh put into servicing his expertise.
Hesitant in ensuring even a one percent chance.
Yet, produced a fraction of the dosage,
Of the substance, Mesode used to administer,
Enemas during pregnancy to stay within the pace
Of growth and development of the baby
And to dispel remains harmful to the body.
Help to strengthen the immune system.
Dressed a semi-cylinder wooden bowl
With clean clothes and capped with a towel
Red camwood applied to his entire body.
Topped with herbs of temperature control
From a piece of plantain leaf, produce a funnel.
In it, warmed herbs, squeezed into the baby's nostrils,
Ears, eyes, and mouth to keep the heart functional,
Regulate respiratory distress and oxygen control.
Wrapped the baby's head with the same herbs
And purple petals of a plantain.
Placed the baby in the wooden bowl and covered
With warmed plantain leaves to prevent contact.

Ma'Ahone assistant solicitation had no limitation
Even those that showed no emotion
Convinced Ejuape won't make it alive
Yet, she didn't stop the pestering for a cure.
After six months of intensive care
Even skeptics began to admit it was time,
To give Ejuape a surviving chance.
Haters, however, didn't think he should live.
Haunted by his deceased mother's memories
They made attempts at his life.

Ma'Ahone incantation petitions weren't deluded.
So did her hard work not go unrewarded.
Standing solidly firm in defense and protection
She deflated any subtle attempt at his elimination.
Ejuape made it alive to the chagrin of doubters.
And admiration of Ma'Ahone's well-wishers.
Ancestral tribute and the Almighty's recognition
Remained the Muane-Ngoe valuable means of appreciation
For a miraculous survival and growth
She planned to celebrate Ejuape's birth.
Though it wasn't in the Muane-Ngoe cultural norm
Reminding people of their birthday, yearly, let alone,
Organized an unanticipated and grandiose
Party for kids and teenagers within his age range.
The Muane-Ngoe people recognize
And are celebrated twice in their lifetime.
During their birth and death, while
They celebrate themselves once,
When they get married.

Concerning Nnam's birthday celebration, Ma'Ahone,
Had in the back of her mind an unavailable goal,
Officially adorn her precious gift,
With a befitting and meaningful first name.
Circumstances surrounding Ejuape's birth
Gave no allowance for a naming ceremony
Being part of the rite performed on the fourth day
Of the birth of every male child.
Ejuape, as a name, was a sobriquet, misfortune indicative.
That tag connotation remained unacceptable,
And bothered Ma'Ahone's joyful psyche.

On her orders, a young man walked the streets;
With a gong and said in a melodious voice
"Kids, toddlers, still crying in their mothers' arms,
Do you pee, pooh, and your mother showers you?
Ma'Ahone's house welcomes you.
If you can walk, run to Ma'Ahone's home
Or children hold your father's hand.
If you can't walk, crawl; if you crawl, children,
Let your mother come with you.
Children of all ages come, come, and celebrate."

One week of preparation to attain the objective,
Summed up to assorted traditional dishes
A cleaned hut and decorated with yellow palm fronds
An assembly of children and elders
With Ejuape in their midst,
A small loincloth passed in between his legs
And fastened around the waist
With red camwood strokes
On his face and chest and assorted beads
Necklace, and strands of yellow palm fronds.
Tied on the elbows and wrists like a prince
Of the ancient Ngeme-Ngoe kingdom
That broke away from the Ngoe dynasty,
Before the advent of slavery.
The Ngeme-Ngoe kingdom itself fractured,
Into upper and lower kingdoms due in part
To natural disasters and land conquest
Which remained the central precept
In the defense, protection, and land acquisition.
Ma'Ahone was in a bright multicolored

Hand embroidered Kaba made from yarn,
With white and black necklace beads.
Gracing the celebration, and a necessary prelude
With a kola nut and the pouring of libation as a start
An elderly person handled that assignment,
Chanted incantations to invoke ancestral presence.

Satisfied that the children ate and drank to their fill.
Ma'Ahone stood in their midst,
And raised her voice, "give me a moment."
Maintaining an agreeable level of silence.
She employed her nightingale voice,
With a stylistic Ngoneh-dance
For two attention-grabbing minutes.
And thrilled the joyous audience.
Taking a deep but exciting breath, she said;
"It was today, four years ago, around this time,
A storm so violent shocked the entire village,
Ravaged property and left many homeless
That Ejuape took a breath so hazardous,
The conditions of his birth were hoped to dampen,
A painstaking nightmare but with supporting
Herbal treatment and ancestors blessing
Two years elapsed to guarantee a son in the making.
This life saving and changing decision,
Makes me a proud mother of a gallant son
Warrior of the ancient Ngeme-Ngoe kingdom.
These circumstances, children, stood in the way,
Of performing a befitting naming ceremony.
Our togetherness, therefore, marks the official naming.
My son from this day shall be known as Nnam.

The children chorused Nnam, Nnam, Nnam.
"Can I hear you say that again, my children?"
Nnam, Nnam, Nnam…they chorused.
Nnam, meaning Blessing, was suitable
For a motherless birth defect child,
The thoughts of survival, being alive
And sound in health was worthy of celebrating.

Strong and ready at the age of four
Running childlike errands for his mother.
Nothing gave Ma'Ahone the delight,
Then watching Nnam roaming the streets,
Walking around, pulling her hand
Jumping up and down in the yard
And enunciating; mother, mother, mother.
Crying, being snobbish, and avoiding strangers.
How wonderful, what fate had denied,
Her for many years, the love of a child.
If nothing else, the feeling of fulfillment,
Having saved a soul in distress meant
Everything and surpassed every accomplishment.

Turning six was a milestone,
The need to upgrade her son to a man,
Became culturally and symbolically compulsory.
In the Bantu cultures and specifically
Within the Muane-Ngoe sub or main proclivity
The performance of a circumcision rite
A compulsory cultural obligation to male kids.
She had no husband, neither
Did Nnam had a father

A male figure was absent in the home.
And circumcision was a rite
Women weren't allowed any involvement
Except the wish to let the male
Undergo the ordained ritual.

Ma'Ahone employed Elumpes' services
The traditional healer whose role
Kept Nnam alive, responsive, and active.
Performing circumcision surgery rites
Constituted part of his traditional practices.
Mornings within the lower Ngeme-Ngoe kingdom
And its precincts were usually chilly
Following the doctor's orders
Ma'Ahone let her son have a cold shower.
To the River Nndum cataract
For purification towards the rite.
Fixed a place behind her home,
Led her son to the kitchen stool,
Facing a panorama of tropical trees
And with a throbbing heart, left the premise.

Still seated, Nnam was agonizing,
Hissing and grunting in anguish.
Haven concluded the rite
Elumpeh and his son took turns
Washing their hands and the surgery equipment.
And behold to their bewilderment,
A white dove flew and alighted on Nnam's head.
You are a benediction," Elumpeh enthused
Nnam kept a stiff neck, staring

At Elumpeh, while the dove turned around, cooing.
Breaking the order, Mama Ahone rushed behind.
To witness that which had astounded Elumpeh,
And triggered Nnam's eulogization.
Gazing at his son in wonderment, the dove flew.
"From your ancestors, your blessings have come.
From the creator, you shall perform miracles.
You shall be a leader of the people.
The one, the ancestors, have chosen."
"Chosen for what purpose?" Ma'Ahone asked.
"He's chosen for great stride
That even me can't define
Greater than anyone can explain
Strides with no defined limitations
And coming from the spirits," Elumpeh replied.

Raising her hands to the sky,
"Behold, I proclaim this day,
In honor of the creator and our ancestry
That he was made a man, twice," Ma'Ahone, said.
Elumpeh declared Nnam healed,
From the surgery, three weeks afterward,
Ma'Ahone killed and prepared a chicken.
Before presenting the dish, she chanted the incantation.
Asked Nnam to kneel, and on his neck
Bestowed a bright blue beats lace
Hung two bleached teeth of a Tigress
With these last solemn and exhorting words,
Handed an ancient spear in the form of a staff.

"The secret to the sacred spirit
Of the Muane-Ngoe people was with a woman.
The men ganged-up and hashing a desperate plot
Made it their partial possession.
And a tool for subjugating, so perfect.
Taking away everything from a woman
Making the greatest gift insignificant
That which God gave the masters of procreation
"The symbol of change, the host
You shall be and for no reason,
And at no cost should you give this out.
In the Ngeme-Ngoe genealogy storyline
These relics make up part
Of the breakaway account from the Ngoe dynasty
Age would give the expository."

The excitingly attractive buzz
Of reverberations emanating from the village arena
Pulled Nnam and her mother
To come and pass the time like other villagers
In community organized Esuwa (wrestling) encounters
Within three different age groupings
And twelve-year-old Nsong was roaring
Humbling and crushing all opponents
To the displeasure of their cheering parents.
Nsong had to the surprised of spectators
Made fifteen-year-old Ekume eat dust
And there seems no challenger left
Within the age group of sixteen to test-fist.
Hopping delightfully in cheering enchantment
They had all curled and wrapped their tails,

In-between their legs in self-defeat like Pangolins.
Little Nnam ignited by the force of adrenaline,
Rose from his mother laps with anxiety
Stretched both hands for defy.
Broking protocol rather than Keng (King) Etubweh
The venerated traditional leader whose death brother
Had been rumored to be Nnam biological father
Hopped towards Elumpeh and stooped.
Elumpeh, like fellow elders, hung on his shoulder
The ngwe-bag and holding a walker.
Stretched his walker and pat Nnam's back.
He rose and staring back at his mother
And their looks coinciding in agreement
She stood and toned a song to fulfill his request.
The crowd cheering following drum beats
Nsong, paced backward then hopped forward
Tenaciously grabbed Nnam and swung
Ferociously for venturing a fighter
Nnam agilely landed like a warrior.
Reaching out, he made a sly backbreaking,
Move that led to Nsong falling.
Raising both hands agonizingly calling,
For help from supporters that kept howling.
A kid with no experience in wrestling,
The community agreed another warrior was in the making.
"A Lion has risen,
An umbrella tree has germinated," Ma'Ahone, enthused.

A week hadn't elapsed since the wrestling encounter
Then, Ma'Ahone began grappling with mounting pressure.
The whisperings of Nnam's ability amongst villagers

Began raising questions about his parentage.
Ma'Ahone observed with consternation,
How even some elders scorned her son.
Understandably, she was aware,
Children with questionable parentage,
Were subjected to bullying to taint the ego.
And made to believe they were being lacked.

It was hot with rumbles of thunder.
Ma'Ahone accompanied her son to the river.
That would make the first time,
Since turning eight, she followed him for a routine.
Walking a few meters within the dry-cracking-foliage
She stopped and leaned on a gigantic Njabe tree.
Staring up the colossal tree pregnant with green fruits
Nnam placed his clay pot on dead leaves.
"When one is born in a society, stratified,
He or she gets easily stigmatized.
I won't be alive and witness my son traumatized.

The Muane-Ngoe people say,
Achievement begets recognition
And recognition begets name.
When an act of valor is linked to a kid
People begin to trace his background.
Your wrestling triumph a fortnight ago
Triggered the crazing lips of conspirators
To salivate over your clouded bloodline.
Both parents being in a child's life
Our people consider it an ideal upbringing.
But the ways of the Almighty are challenging.

Such a pattern of living isn't practicable,
In all family settings and households
Because fate separates mother from father
Father from children and mother
Even children from both parents
Parentage dynamics possess no fixed determinant,
Even when mastered religiously,
With all the laydown rules of life.
When it rains, it falls on everyone's roof.

My son, whether it's both parents as we desire it.
One parent as we can tolerate it
Or no parent at all as we dislike it.
Circumstances may differ with contorted pathways
But human beings follow the same trajectory
To attain the concrete goals of life.
Therefore, let the absence of a father
I tell you today, not be a source of despair.
What becomes of a child without a mother,
Children without any family members?
You share the same gift with everybody.
The gift of life by the almighty.
How you make use of that divine aptitude,
Depends not on your background and people
But on the belief that no matter the mire,
What the creator has made of you
No one can take it away from you."

Pulling Nnam, she stepped away, facing the tree.
"Look straight at the tree; do you see through it.
Or that which is behind it?" Ma'Ahone asked.

"Ma, that's impossible," Nnam replied.
Absolutely, that impossibility isn't limited
To this tree, but extended to human behavior.
Because the content of one's mind is unpredictable
To see beyond that tree, you move to it,
Vacate your standing position or get assistance
Since the impossibility of being in two places
At the same time, it is indisputable and
Even with the best eyesight, human visibility is limited.
To create an impact, you don't walk in isolation.
As huge as the njabe tree is, other trees surround it
People make others great.
Be kind and peaceful if you want to be full of fruits.
And as long and gigantic as this Njabe tree.
Every word coming out of your mouth
Would be as useful and medicinal
As the tree and oil from its nuts.
Avoid hurting others because a wound heals,
The scars are indelible to the victims.
Never rush to judgment even when the truth
Seems glaring, you be like a one-legged
Walking on a slippery path.
Be a ratel instead of a lion.
Don't have the heart of a king.
In a position of power, they have no mercy,
Of those that challenge their wisdom.
They don't mind burying the truth.
Even if everyone would die
For them to stay in power.
The evil ones die suddenly and mysteriously.
If they have to die old

They won't die until
Ancestors have made them sit,
In the pool and smell of their shit.

The poignant lore Ma'Ahone poured out,
Gave Nnam dithers as tears rolled down his eyes
"Oh, my sunlight," she stretched her hands out
Grabbed Nnam for a warm, soothing embrace.
"What grief troubles your heart?"
"Is there going to be a tomorrow for you and me?
The picture in my mind is not so bright.
Although full of wisdom indicates the precipice
Of a foreboding mother to bow out," he replied
"Ancestors always look to our future.
Be confident; it's not dark for me yet.
As you dance the dance of life
Full of thorns and undesired outcomes
Your Mother will always dance alongside you.
Because, we say when it's bad, it returns to the owner.
My position is explained in this Muane-Ngoe,
Classic rhetoric upbringing song
What cleans a house? A broom,
No matter how you devote time
In the upbringing of someone's child,
If you fail to nourish yours,
Your efforts go in vain.

The love story between Ma'Ahone
And Nnam was too delicious and delicate,
Consequential and inspiring to last a long time.
An unpredictable tragedy interrupted the course.

Giving her no time to live the divine providence
She witnessed bestowed upon her son.
Then, misfortune alternatively, predestination,
Settled in-between in the most abrupt way.
So it happened again, and painfully
That which befell Nnam at birth
Called again, with Ma'Ahone's untimely death.
Exactly at Nnam's ninth birthday,
From an unspecified illness, nontraumatic, the least,
To think it could claim her involving life.

Fate may have denied Nnam the bond,
With his birth mother. Living the repercussions
Of the attenuating loss and setbacks.
Yet, as sudden and unexpected as the challenges,
Were at birth, they didn't turn out disastrous.
Despite the anguish and birth defects.
Amidst trials, he made it alive,
Outliving every anticipated conjecture.
Better than some toddlers with both parents
In the same household and with no birth defects.
Nevertheless, even at the teenage age of nine,
Ma'Ahone abrupt death produced an unquantifiable
Impact on Nnam's well-being and life.
With traumatic nightmares, the loss came.
The most wrecking being the revelation
Ma'Ahone, not being his birth mother
Commiserate that his birth took away his mother.
As a juvenile, as he was, the anguish of the lost,
His pending destiny falling into strange
Hands predictably became unavoidable.

Neither the poverty level nor wealth possession
By the Foster or adoptive parents determine
The predilection towards an orphan
The Muane-Ngoe people warn.
The free will of benevolence, parents
Voluntarily display towards the orphan,
Irrespective of a myriad of challenges
Born from the decision to accept responsibility,
Of being in the life of needy children.

When favor doesn't belie; Orphans
Have compassionate and mindful relations.
Some more sympathetic and forbearing
Others bully and remain unbending.
When unfortunate, no one zeros in on,
They live in the streets and feed on leftovers,
And sometimes, visit people's bins.
The fate that follows countless Orphans
Befell Nnam, in every measure, squarely
He wasn't better than the legendary
Muane-Ngoe orphan who fed
Off leftovers of bones and sour food
Not good for human consumption.

As a teenage boy, Nnam was forced,
To do chores at very odd times,
Under duress and in perilous situations,
Even under inclement and cruel weather
When everyone else was home, lazily.
More frustrating was the insistence

Of having to repeat assignments without need.
Overwhelmed by the pressure of hatred and
Mistreatment, when he got to the stream,
At times, sat down and cried his eyes out,
Recalling the wonderful moments he shared
With Ma'Ahone weeping and
Waiting, imagining she could appear
To him, like the Nfo-Ngoe River Bird,
Whose mother went in search of food
The little bird perched by the riverside
Singing an endless lullaby.
Wailing and waiting, not knowing
His mother had been trapped.
And would never return no matter how he waited,
And wept because she had died.

As empty as an empty space
Who has put off the light on me,
The Almighty or the ancestors?
No one has two mothers
But I did, and alas,
None is here with me.
Where do I go from here?
Abandoned, me, who do I name
For my silence and misfortune
On whose shoulder do I mourn?

Standing in the trail of the ancestors,
No one does, not even the evil spirits,
The Muane-Ngoe people caution.
Although Nnam was malnourished

He grew tall, muscular, assiduous, and animated.
And fit in the usage of the epigram,
When God allows scabies to infest a child
He also provides fingernails to the child.
Made a tool for the drudgery
He cut grass, dug stumps, cut trees,
And till the soil, even passed twilight.
And resumed at the crack of dawn.
Routinely guarded goats and sheep
At night from Panthers and Leopards
Prevent them from being devoured in the dead
Of the night when everyone else had slept
Sometimes without Bow and Arrow, but
Thanks to the relic Ma'Ahone left
In his keeping, it became a tool so great
For self-defense and protection, despite attempts
From villagers, including Keng Etubweh
To make the spear part of his royal possession.
Remarkably, anytime he guarded these animals,
Through the nights or was at a pasturage,
Two spirits accompanied his every move.
Dreaming and seeing visions in the entourage
Of two women giving him directives
Standing to the fore of danger.
And the riskiest of situations.
Chastisements and attacks were habitually
Meted out to taint his ego
Returning early from the farm and at the same time,
As everyone did, it was a crime.
Running errands beyond his age.
And under much draconian living conditions.

Assignments with the toughest measure of endurance
Yet, no matter the challenges
Before him, the tasks were met
Many times to the chagrin and displeasure
Of the narcissistic host and relations
Such treatment gave birth to miscreants
With the desire to go astray
Soil their conduct and name
In most cases, and from time to time
Maybe forced to undertake
Or get involved in a life of crime.
Nnam got tempted countless times
With enticing and lucrative proposals
Of rubbery, broke in and purloining
Nevertheless, consciously stayed out of trouble
In every tainting attempt to rope him.

Seventeen was still a budding age,
Yet, Nnam was sated and done
Living with Elder Esambe, uncle Ekane
And aunty Nzugeh, all of whom claimed
Relationship with Mesode and well as Ma'Ahone.
Stepping out of the cage
That made him both a prisoner of conscience,
And undue torture.
Abused and starved even when he did no wrong.
And so he began wondering
If these evil acts meted out
On him daily like a delinquent
Were for the pains and misery his parents
Allegedly inflicted on fellow villagers?

Even if these charges were affirmative
How could torturing him be justified?
Being punished for the sins of his mother
Not very much he knew about Mesode,
Except for rumor-mongering and hearsay
About the impact of her negative earthly life.
And by extension, perhaps those of his father.
He had no knowledge and background.
No idea how he lived within his family and beyond
Not much he knew about Ma'Ahone as a kid.
To believe she was too evil to be maligned,
An outcast for him to be mistreated.
He had almost become one-legged,
From an untreated bullwhip injury.

The streets like his relatives' homes
Were devoid of compassion and kindness
Moving, self-educating from place to place,
To give his life a meaningful existence
Making the Almighty and his ancestors
Codes of conduct, his precious companions.
He studied grasses and roots, herbs and trees,
As well as animals and birds.
He mastered their names and sounds.
Could determine the weather and atmospheric conditions.
Listening to the whispering of wind and singing of birds.

Quickly, and to the amazement of detractors
Became an engaging participant in gatherings.
No matter the group and subject
Provided the motive was to exalt,

The supernatural and acknowledge his descent.
Mastering the wisdom of his pedigree
And earnestly practicalize the creed.
Sounding sometimes like a representation of the doctrine,
The early British Missionaries were preaching in the hinterlands.
Better still a pupil of the council of Nicaea
Before the New wave of the Berlin Order
Permeating Africa that made divine
The son of man, even when his mother,
Was way distant and nothing close,
To the propagated immaculate mother.
And his parentage had no link to the patriarch,
Of this Bantu tribe and flock
That could produce a breed with such sapience.
Nevertheless, in him, there were signs.
In him, there seems to be answers.
Even when everyone thought nothing better
Could come out of a pauper.

Progressively bestowed upon him by the ancestors.
And with the seal of approval by the creator.
Began to demonstrate the collective wisdom of a leader
And the proficiency of a traditional healer.
He seemed poised as a challenger
Of conventional wisdom and ideology
To dish out refined knowledge in spirituality.
A purpose-driven man, despite the agony,
And understanding the power of the Almighty.
Street pressure couldn't derail his force of personality.
With an unbending zeal of channeling his messages

To his ancestors, converting his starving periods,
To fasting and healing his mind.
Questioning the rationale for his existence
The truth surrounding his mothers' exit,
And what became of their departed spirits.
He meditated fervently to have an understanding,
Of the after-death mystery, particularly an encounter
That would make the ancestor lead him to the creator.

Gradually Nnam put behind the past,
As he advanced in age and thought.
And had fully embraced his fate,
That everyone had a destined path
When followed to the letter, the quest
For knowledge and predestined intent
With steadfastness were attainable.
He had never hoped of becoming a healer.
Neither a traditional theologian, however,
If that were what destiny had allotted,
He was more than ready in all respects,
To embrace the challenge with every might.

Knowledge of traditional medicine and
The process of it was never limited,
To specific individuals and family background.
From one clan and household to another
Each had the discernment to concoct herbs,
Share diagnosis and their prescriptive dosage.
Understanding that herbal knowledge collectivism
Fostered the healing and curative processes
Instead of isolated individual performance.

The range of knowledge transfer
Healing acquired through learning
Or the process of inheritance and
That conveyed through ancestral necromancy
Were different in methodology and adroitness.
Even in healing, the efficacy was distinguishable.
In the event of an epidemic spate
The personal and collective contribution
On rare occasions, few individuals discriminated,
In adeptness and efficacy
The likes of Elumpeh and Nnam
To earn the admiration of accomplished healers.
Nevertheless, to attain Elumpeh's ranks,
Nnam out of the ordinary,
Gave a new meaning to traditional medicine
By performing a visual enteroscopy.
What Elumpeh considered a miracle
On one of his kidney patients
Who happened to be Senge, the king's daughter.
Elumpeh like other villagers through diagnostics
Could determine a kidney patient
And provide immediate treatment.
But no one had the proficiency,
To determine if one or both kidneys,
Had deteriorated and the extent of the deterioration.
Nnam put water in a semicylinder calabash.
Squeeze some herbs into it
Including a red coloration produced
From a garden-egg-like wild fruit.
On Nnam's orders, Senge stood
By the calabash and stooped

To wash her face and hands.
Placing her right hand on her stomach
And Nnam holding her left hand, upon rising,
The anterior of her anatomy
Displaced in the calabash to Elumpeh's stupefaction.

Born in an era when culture and tradition
Experience a high level of stratification
Young men with an unrecognized background
Were denied initiation into various masquerades
That constituted the symbol of social influence.
A channel through which educational values
Were passed on even to the least privileged kids.
But with his newly acquired healing powers,
Villagers instantly saw the need to initiate,
And upgrade his status in the rank and file,
Of all masquerades that embodied the code
Of conduct as the people viewed and understood.
The circumstances of Nnam's birth had denied,
The adornment of these sobriquets, thus, he declined,
To accept that which he had been disqualified.

Over ten centuries ago, all dynasties and kingdoms
From Central to East Africa born of the Bantu ancestry
Possessed similar genealogical and agrarian characteristics.
Like most others, the collapse of the Ngoe Dynasty,
Was due in part to a lack of strong leadership.
The unwillingness to be led by a single warring personality
Or the absence of warlord characters.
The avoidance of violence and patrimony
Through the use of arms for territorial acquisitions

Influenced the rise of kingdoms the bulk tributary
As well as secondary kingdoms.
In the aftermath of European imperialism and autocracy
Debased to chiefdoms.
Resulting in significant territorial disputes
Amongst the Ngoe progeny.
Clans rising against each other,
Villages attacked and dispersed citizens.
Some were captured and held prisoners.
Tribal polarization and cultural affiliations,
Arose out of such discontent and mistreatments.
By the end of the 13th century, the Ngoe Dynasty
Had fully fractured in no less than nine tribal kingdoms
By the time the slave trade began, the dispersion
Hadn't only increased but led to the loss
Of some tribes of Ngoe's descendance.

At the time of Nnam's call,
The ownership of the Esemewo waterfall.
Located at the foot of the now, Mbakwa Supe Rocky Hill,
Of the River Wa(e) (Mongo), which constitutes the longest stretch
Separating and uniting the Nfo-Ngoe (Bafaw),
Mukunda-Ngoe (Bakundu) From Ngeme-Ngoe (Bakossi)
And Mboe-Ngoe (Bakossi) kingdoms
Was among one of such disputes
Known to be the last battles
Pitching the Mukunda-Ngoe and the Ngeme-Ngoe kingdoms.
Twice, the Mukunda-Ngoe had put in place,
A formidable force having been subjected to a tough battle.

Before Nnam became a household name
The second encounter put no scare in the minds,
Of the opponent that proved unsubmissive.
The Mukunda-Ngoe with the advance knowledge
The Ngeme-Ngoe were battle-ready and fierce.
Even though numerically few,
Assembled a larger army of young men
Regrouped and encamped in the slopes
And valleys within the waterfall slab.

Not oblivious of their opponent resilience
The Lower-Ngeme-Ngoe community heads
Led by Keng (King), Etubweh consulted Nnam.
Keng Etubweh and his Ngwe (Council) kinsmen
Were shocked at Nnam's declaration.
Tracing the relationship with the Mukunda-Ngoe
He favored the pursuance of peace
Advocated negotiating the occupancy of the landmass.
For farming and fishing purposes and agree to share
The usage of the waterfall and the River Wa (Mongo).
The seven villages of the Lower Ngeme-Ngoe kingdom
With Elder Esambe as the masquerades head
Disappointed, all rejected the recommendations.
And persuaded Keng Etubweh to issue a declaration,
Accept an offer from the Upper Ngeme-Ngoe,
Kinsmen who had more than two hundred young men
Trained in the act of the Muane-Ngoe warfare
Mastered the skill of Danegun artillery
The massive production of gunpowder.
To be conscripted into the Lower Ngeme-Ngoe defense.
To match the Mukunda-Ngoe huge fighting force.

Keng Etubweh dabbled with the suggestion.
Summoned Elumpeh to back the initiative.
Elumpeh lauded the move but warned against it.
Opposing Nnam spelled immediate ruination.

After forty years of rule, the king, like his predecessor
Let his people in three battles and won
In all the confrontations, no seer mounted such opposition
And stood against the acquisition of more land.
Nnam's decision was beyond the king's understanding.
Almost three weeks it took villagers assessing,
The decision behind Nnam's rejection
Before Keng Etubweh sought the assistance
Of Motale-Wa-Nganda, a Mukunda-Ngoe elder
Nnam had cured of goiter.
Motale-Wa-Nganda hitherto becoming sick,
Was the emissary and thinker for the Mukunda-Ngoe.

The Mukunda-Ngoe were no sleeping dogs
Swung into action immediately Motale-Wa-Nganda
Presented Keng Etubweh's agenda.
The Sesse Nopanjo (sub-kings) of the Mukunda-Ngoe
Chanting the Nyamkpe masquerade war song
Rallied men of valor before the Nganga Mataka (supreme
leader or king)
Whose birth names were Moto-Watobi Lenya.
The Nganga Mataka, stepped out of his woody hut.
His dimple hairy face was bright.
A staff embroiled with the mane of a tiger and
A keg of palm wine in his hands.
"I see the enthusiasm in the eyes of every warrior.

And I ask, shall the Mukunda-Ngoe…
Succumb to the whims of Ngeme-Ngoe?
The Etuma people, we are twice their population.
As the warriors listened, he poured libation.
The land of our forefathers is in contention.
Sons and daughters of Ngoe,
And we shall not allow any Ngoe progeny,
To slight us out of the land of our ancestors.
We come a long way with the Etumas.
Yet, we wouldn't permit them to sit on our dignity.
The Mukunda-Ngoe broke away from the Ngoe dynasty,
Not out of cowardice but a valiance ability
The desire to conquer, establish and thrive.
All Ngoe sons followed the same course,
In the vast landmass to establish their dominance.

The Mukunda-Ngoe dismissed every proposal,
Motale-wa-Nganda advanced to convince his people,
Going to war, again and at this time was futile.
The risk of losing with Nnam's power
Potions of land already occupied was greater.
The Ngeme-Ngoe stood a better chance,
Of overrunning them in battle.

The Mukunda-Ngoe weren't different in approach.
Having the same cultural affinity and pedigree
Convinced in their warrior's ability and preparedness,
And with a strategy mapped out a plan.
Summoned their most gifted traditional healers
For divination and spiritual fortification.
Like the Ngeme-Ngoe, the Mukunda-Ngoe believed

That a battle is fought twice,
First in the spiritual realm
Through the cosmic energy of ancestral necromancy
Before the physical participation, which is the combination
Of combat preparedness and exertion of prowess.

The Nganga Mataka underscored Motale-wa-Nganda's
contribution.
Waited for him to deliver the Mukunda-Ngoe's repudiation.
Wondering what would be Nnam's reaction
Keng Etubweh summoned his kinsmen.
They were still to attend their leader,
When news of the Mukunda-Ngoe attack on farmers
Broke, overshadowing every other activity.
The warriors let by Masoma-Wa-Linonge,
A crown prince born and raised
In the tributary Kingdom of Itoki.
His mother was credited to be the leader.
Of the dreaded Maloba-women secret cult.
No warrior in the Mukunda-Ngoe bloodline
Demonstrated skillful ability in combat
And helped the Mukunda-Ngoe in land acquisition,
Then the five feet tall Masoma-Wa-Linonge.
Camping in the slab and slopes of the waterfall
They had moved and laid in ambush,
Within the peripheries of the Ngeme-Ngoe farmstead.
Confused by the outcry and number of casualties
A pandemonium set into the communities
Like leopards invading a tribe of goats at night.
The Ngeme-Ngoe warriors assembled at Nnam's hut.
Elder Esambe had a few but poignant words.

"A dog has bitten us on the head.
Two tortoises before us, both are female.
I wouldn't throw the blame on where we felt,
Which is Nnam for dissuading the community.
I would instead blame where we slid,
Which is Keng Etubweh for his failure
To stamp his feet on the ground,
By rejecting combat assistance from Upper-Ngemengoe,
And thereby preventing a preemptive battle,
That could have curbed the Mukunda-Ngoe firepower."
Nnam came out of the oracle hut with his staff spear.
"It's another terrible day
In the Ngoes' history
The Mukunda-Ngoe have embraced war
And rejected the olive branch
Pushing the Ngeme-Ngoe on a defensive.
However, I refuse to declare
A full-scale battle,
And maintain the previously held position.
We can't make our brothers our enemies.
We shall go all out to force them to retreat.
I was a warrior before I became a healer.
And understanding the outcome of battling one another,
I request we proceed with caution."

Edisobe, the Ngeme-Ngoe lead warrior
Holding a Danegun stepped forward.
"My fellow warriors, custodians of our land
Goats are eating our palm-tree on the head.
We can't be under a vicious ambush,
And Nnam is professing nonaggression.

How do we cautiously fight armed warriors?
Going by traditional norms
I don't know any healer and seer,
Of the Muane-Ngoe creed
Who undermines some aspect of his culture.
By declining all masquerades initiation,
Nnam is like a basket that can't hold water.
We are talking about a pending battle,
Part of our land is already under siege.
And you leave behind our masquerade,
Which is the source of our strength.
All because amongst us are women.
I, Edisobe, a bonafide warrior
And haven undertook all masquerade initiations
I move that Nnam being part of the warring team,
It will affect our performance. And I see us,
In the next few days succumbing to the Mukunda-Ngoes.

Had Edisobe committed an abomination
Questioning Nnam's commitment as the custodian of the
tradition?
Or was he justifiably right in his accusation.
On these allegations, Nnam faced multiple factions.
By rejecting initiation, Nnam was rejecting tradition.
Therefore, many backed Edisobe's motion.
How would a man call himself
The Oracle of the ancestors
Yet, rejects the very core of his identity? They argued.

There's excrement on the village crossbeam.
Its repugnant odor constitutes a nightmare.

Villagers must clean before anyone walks on it again.
Unfortunately, we have a rope on our neck.
We preferably walk past it now.
And redress the mess we made afterward.
For the impending challenge is more repulsive
Than the mere excrement smell," Elder Esambe said.

"Woohoo! I hear repetitive strange sounds,
Like raindrops over the roof of the house.
Our land is under invasion, our safety,
Threatened, and all we do is question the loyalty,
Of the one, we anticipate leading the battle.
No one wants to roast plantains,
And in the process, burns his fingers.
Have the Mukunda-Ngoe bewitched us?
Edisobe's concerns are at the nucleus,
Of the foundation of our traditional beliefs.
We have an unhatched egg in our hands.
Throw it away; instead, I recommend,
Rather than have it broken," Keng Etubweh responded.

Nnam pinned his spear on the ground.
"If there are more unhatched eggs
I declare this moment, a time to break them.
I can stand the smell they will emit.
Edisobe can question my traditional commitment.
But questioning my citizenship adherence,
With impunity is a little unfortunate.
I wouldn't blame him because he doesn't understand
One can be scared of a caged and fed lion.
Or as we say, an arrow shot in anger,

Falls in-between the shooter's legs.
These warriors standing here
Are within my age range.
They had undertaken before fifteen
All key masquerades initiation rites
That form, the basis of our cultural beliefs.
Why wasn't I part of these initiations?
Was I less of a citizen
When they granted entrance to everyone else?
I was an unqualified fatherless adolescent.

How did I become qualified?
In the early days of my adulthood?
In the rank and file of the highest masquerade
When from the lowest ranks I was rejected.
Did I stop being a fatherless child?
No, but you elders, recognized to your displeasure
That the ancestors' light had shone on me.
The one some of you, wished dead.
As Ma'Ahone told me, what the ancestors
And the Almighty had made you.
No one can take it away from you.

If the consensus is that initiating me
Will establish relevance in my practice
Which as an oracle of the ancestors is insignificant
For there's no better, stronger, and more mystery
Initiation than the process I have undergone
Through the uninterrupted leadership of the ancestors.
I shall definitely embrace it for our culture.
However, as it's said, when a man's house is on fire,

He doesn't chase rats.
We are facing an unprecedented strike
From an opponent, we can't underestimate.
The Mukunda-Ngoe kingdom is huge
Their fighting force outnumbers us.
We don't have any means to determine
The aggressor's level of preparedness and resistance.
Therefore, Edisobe and his faction must understand
We all have varying gifts and abilities.
And only collective force can subdue the Mukunda-Ngoe.

Had Nnam underestimated the Mukunda-Ngoe's
resoluteness?
For four days, they put up a relentless
Display of warring prowess.
From one village and farmland to another
Victory seeming imminent,
They called for reinforcement.
Scampering for their safety
Villagers began to desert their community.
All attempts to compel them to recede,
Met the toughest defiance
The Ngeme-Ngoe have faced,
In any battle since breaking away
From the seat of the Ngoe Dynasty.
The Ngeme-Ngoe warriors being overpowered,
Laid Nnam's reputation on the line.
Since becoming a healer, for the first time,
He panicked and retreated home.
Leaving other warriors in active battle.

The appearance of Nnam at the community entrance
Alone looking weary and trounce
Provoked an unanticipated disturbance.
Walking towards the village arena
Women and children rushed, lamenting
And wailing in anguish, concluding
The other warriors hadn't survived the Mukunda-Ngoe
onslaught…
No one expressed surprise and disappointment
Like Keng Etubweh, thinking Nnam was out
To ruin his reign and pitch him against his people.

"What else is left to say
Edisobe's prophecy may be coming to a realization.
The Mukunda-Ngoe have eaten the Elephant excrement.
Their Hen is laying eggs,
And our land is gradually besieged," Keng Etubweh
admonished.
"Not all eggs a Hen lays are hatched.
The unhatched will never become chicks.
They are a waste and can't either be consumed...
Elders of the Ngeme-Ngoe, my fellow country people.
I hope there's a Mukunda-Ngoe elder,
Among us, or son and daughter.
If there's none, I plead with you all,
Take the message to them.
Our warriors are still on the battlefield.
Our land is on fire.
But we must trace the steps of our ancestors.

I may have been misled into believing

We are in a season of reawakening.

A period when all sons and daughters of Ngoe

The length and breadth of the Muane-Ngoe territory

From the salty waters of Bimbia to the Idabato estuary

From the Korup dense forest to the Mbo-Bayang sanctuary

From the Balue Hills to the Ligbea Mountain

From the creeks of Keka to the Kupe Mountain

From the Mwangem twin lakes to the Barombi lake.

Understanding fighting and suppressing each other is unprofitable.

The more we fight, the further peace eludes us.

Growth will be like a tortoise journey.

And the dispersion of our people,

To unknown and unreachable lands will remain steady.

We can't be our own enemy.

Being confrontational with the Mukunda-Ngoe,

We have been before and gained nothing but animosity.

The Ngeme-Ngoe have acquired a huge landmass.

From no one else but our progeny.

In the process, we lost countless lives.

Of what use is the abundant territory

With this dwindling population?

I supplicated our ancestors to shadow,

Our willingness to battle.

Wandering the forest and deflating every possible strike.

I caught up with Masoma-Wa-Linonge.

And told him we lack the enthusiasm to battle.

That we no longer favor combatting one another.

In hope, the Mukunda-Ngoe would call a truce.

But passed grievances have darkened their minds.

They have refused to reason past revenge.

Preferring to build a web instead of a nest.
I have returned to reverse the course,
Of our previously held position.
At which point in our lives do we absolutely
Envision we shall come together, again,
As a people who shared the same ancestry?

By the third cockcrow of the ninth day,
No Mukunda-Ngoe warrior came close,
To the Valley and waterfall slab.
Losing all parcels of land
That had been in contention,
Since both sides began to contest ownership
Of the River Wa for farming and fishing.

The battle may have ended,
In favor of the Ngeme-Ngoe
But the number of casualties on both sides,
Told a despicable story, an experience
Nnam as a propagator of peace
Declined to be part of any festivity.
Even though welcomed with a celebrative
And conqueror Ebenzu-war songs.
The cock has crowed and
Everywhere there's commotion.
The king tree that stands out alone.
The unbeatable king of the jungle.

Nnam's emergence to the healing pinnacle
With distinctive characteristics was a puzzle.
Combining traditional theology, necromancer

And cultural savvy coincided with a tall order.
The institutionalization of new beliefs tenets
With the incursion of the British missionaries
In the hinterlands that followed unbendingly
The dismantling of the African continent.
The ramifications of the detestable dispersion
Masterminded by the Ottoman Empire,
Assumed by the Europeans and taken over by America,
The Slave trade had left no African kingdom, Empire, or
Dynasty unaffected.

Gripped by this period of sangfroid
Unanticipated events had overshadowed
The values and norms of the people.
From North to West, the Songhai empire
Had collapsed partly due to the Arabs
Sought control of its extensive wealth,
Weakening its central authority
Controlled communities and landmass.
From Central to East and South,
Kingdoms outfaced rapidly
Monarchies and Dynasties faced challenges.
As political chaos and civil wars took over
The Judar Pasha invasion disintegrated,
Them into groups of smaller kingdoms
By extension, liberated many tributary states,
Having been the source of slaves
For the Tran-Saharan trade routes.
The scheme to disintegrate the giant African
Empires and kingdoms by the European
Were hatched, elaborated, and carried out speedily

In a grand plot entitled, brilliantly;
The Partition of Africa.
Presumably, claiming ownership,
Of a continent, they had no relationship.

The buying and selling with cowries
Phased out with the impositions of new forms
Of exchange and currencies
Making the trade by batter obsolete.
The land was hardly the finest as before
Not vast, and not as fertile
Having been invaded and partitioned by strangers
And with foreign values taking over.
Thriving and attractive centers
Where merchants gathered to trade
Completely dilapidated and in ruins.
The economy of clan systems
Gradually began to fracture.
Even more devastating was the ceaseless
Violent conflicts within organized groups
Same cultures, societies, and nationalities
Giving rise to diseases, manifestations,
Social dysfunction and distress.
Besides, extended periods of droughts
Within the Sahel and Savanna lands
Dealt a blow to most of the small kingdoms
Having a tremendous impact on the ecosystem.
The new order that came to civilize
On its arrival, it instead brought disorientation.
People and communities battled for directions
To accommodate the new pronouncements

That was a draconian, ironfisted antagonist
And dehumanizing to be admired by the host.
The increasing need for a political and economic upsurge
As well as a socio-cultural and traditional course, rose.
That of spiritual leadership and guidance
To communities became even more imperative.
The new religions had begun impacting social life
Breaking down cultural and traditional beliefs
Pitching the old over the young generation.

The Ngeme-Ngoe tributary kingdom
That had moved away from the nucleus,
Muane-Ngoe authority of the Ngoe Dynasty,
Had hardly produced a breed with such energy
In both physical prowess and mental ability
Demonstrating a drive of prophetic nuances
Instilled by the creator and ancestors.
Nnam became an instant crowd-puller.
Appealing to both distress and joyful souls.
His discuss constituted the main catalyst
To understanding his intuitive delimitations
Easing comprehension, believable, and trustworthiness.

Having a mastery of the people's ancestry
Socio-cultural background and genealogy
Remained at the center of his practice.
He was gifted in wisdom,
And refused to allow the refreshed European incursion,
That came with changes in social life,
To derail his thought process,
And pull him away from his ancestral practices.

Though not ignorant of the impacting benefits
The new order represented its lifechanging systems,
In governance, and alterations in cultural values.
Even more appealing was the promise of hope
Through the new religions that emphasized everlasting life,
And paradise as obligatory tenets.

An advocate of benevolence and neighborliness
In every domain and given situations.
Enjoining the elders to be peace lovers,
Stay away from diabolical practices,
And use their talents for community service.
Rather than engage in evil wiles.
Encouraging them to preserve and
Pass on their gifts for societal welfare,
For that sake, God created them.
Nothing of God's creation, he maintained
Was evil and bad, unless manmade.
Therefore, it was as bad as sinning,
The rejection of putting into usefulness
Any of God's creation and creature
All were created for a purpose,
The service of mankind.

Being endowed with these qualities
Made him no special personality
Within the circle of elders.
He neither isolated nor secluded himself
Their experiences were an added value
In learning and the mastery of culture.
So, he made dotage Elumpeh,

His mentor, as well as his contact point.
Elumpeh was gratified that his prophecy,
Had not only seen the break of day,
But it was absolutely valuable.
An eye-opener and a teaching era
To every community that was going to fall
Under the dominance of the renewed European incursion.

The wet season was giving way
Being a major obstacle for outsiders
To explore the hinterlands routinely
And the news that a group of missionaries,
Would make their way to their locality
Had begun to reach villagers' doorsteps.
As recently noticed, such news created anxiety.
Elders were eager to confirm the source waves.
Where Nnam stood and if he had a strategy
Dealing with the prevailing invasive approaches
That was destabilizing their ancestry,
Fracturing traditions and putting a knife
Into their way of life and authority.

Do we not say;
"When a community welcomes a stranger
The community also accepts the stranger's values.
One doesn't accept a visitor into his home,
And deny the visitor a livelihood.
However, these strangers are more than ordinary.
Their mindset is different and full of ambiguity.
Coming from a complex and uneasy environment
Far from what we know, agreed to, and orientated.

And a disposition in beliefs we don't recognize.
Besides, what they have come with
Is a new practical belief system
Everyone is compelled to be part of this engagement,
No matter who you are, where you come from
And what you believe in as a Blackman.
How do you offer a farmer a machete?
And confiscate his farm in exchange?
Do we like and believe in such an approach?
These questions, I leave them to the elders.
And every one of you to provide answers."

"We are as far to the answers,
As their land is far from us," Elumpeh replied.

"We may never understand these people,
With a different psyche and culture.
Our belief system is fundamentally different
Both in cultural and theological expression.
Membership of our masquerade society
For instance, it is an act of social responsibility.
Every male is entitled and expected,
To partake in this inclusive society.
Yet, it remains an individual decision and choice.
This phenomenon of duress
Obligating everyone to their beliefs
Is such a strange approach to life
We may never get out of it."

"The Whiteman is a snake with two heads.
Containing both contagious and poisonous substances

We desire and hate simultaneously.
We didn't invite them,
Neither can we reject them.
We don't have what it takes,
To say no, and hold on to that decision.
As long as it takes and we wish
To hope that we could send them away.
That approach in this epoch is uninspiring,
Having been powerless for decades
In the face of the dehumanizing slave trade.
Nevertheless, the need for a cautious embrace,
It isn't only now, but with the coming generations.
We can't like some of the things they have to offer
And hate what they represent completely.
Admittedly, we are in a transitional era.
Where new, foreign values and norms
Are systematically taking over
Disruptive of our long-existing
Laid down codes of conduct and ways of life.
As the white man continues to penetrate the hinterlands
The battle to fight to maintain our core values
Should remain ceaseless and continuous,
It's a crisis for today's generations and those unborn.

A thirst and lack of water leads to a search
Its none availability is intolerable
And pushes us to crush whatever obstacles
Be they hills to ascend or valleys to descend
Not only for our thirst-quenching necessity
But most importantly, our sustainability.
We cultivate the land for food

Body nourishment and spirit preservation.
The land was never asked to be cultivated.
When we are sick, the herbs,
And the traditional doctor doesn't run to us,
Neither do they seek our whereabouts?
Going in the scout of wants and desires
Such are the ways of life.
Anyone in need goes into the forage.
Staying on the spot where we were born
Ruminating would soon be an outdated practice.
Because something new is always worth learning
Worth knowing and worth having.
And one can hardly stay on the spot,
With this changing world and be satisfied.
Therefore, staying where we were born
Would become more challenging
Should we not be able to meaningful change
And transform what we have for the better.
And for everyone to partake in our inheritance.
If we have any hopes for future generations
It should be a cardinal goal.
Of those who have no movement need
The white people need something,
They desire what we have more than
They have a willingness to offer.
Being in search of wants
They have to overcome obstacles
Traveling the seas and rivers
Ascend and descend hills and valleys
Their desire for our ancestral endowment.
Is the drive behind their endurance.

When a woodpecker leaves the Temperate
And lands in the Tropic, it molds.
Countrymen, don't be fooled
Did you show them the way?
No, you didn't, and no one did
No one ever does to people in need.

When needs and wants are scarce
Desires to step out of the bounds increase
Arming and seeking avenues to overcome
The challenges become a daily routine.
These people have what it takes,
To find their way, anywhere and always.
Improvising and imposing on the hosts.

"How do we overcome these challenges
Now that they are invading every interior
In the land of our ancestry?
Least we neglect, after decades of slavery,
We are licking the wounds of dehumanization."
Worried Elder Esambe, asked.

The Leopard and Deer don't see eye to eye
But when it's the dry season,
They both drink from the same stream.
If all parrots eat from the same plum tree,
They will soon face starvation.
If the Tiger can invade the Leopards territory
Nothing stops the Leopard from getting to the Tiger's lair.
Again, if Wolves can reach a strand of Hyenas.
What stops the Hyenas from visiting a pack of Wolves?

We can't sit on the spot complaining.
And not wanting to seek to understand
Their drive as well as their whereabouts.
The dignity of man
Is linked to his battles of life.
For a cobra to grow big
It must swallow other cobras.
Realistically, not an encouraging approach
To life because it interferes
Into the foundation of human existence.
The social fabric of our pedigree, besides,
Give no allowance for the Blackman
To walk and leave his shadow behind.
However, the Whiteman psyche as humans,
Is different and fits in the cobra's maxim.
Their environment and historical background
Tells a story we must never forget,
And align to no matter the situation.

A grain of corn doesn't turn
Into a cob of maize overnight.
Even on a fertile soil
When planted, it must be nurtured
And follow growth propagation.
For all these, don't let go of your culture.
It's an identity like no other.
Treat it as you nurture a grain of corn.
Dignity, dignity cultural dignity,
That must be safeguarded at all costs.
Don't let go of your beliefs.
Don't let go of your knowledge.

But let go of your evil ways.
Let go of your diabolic psych,
Let the love of your ancestors,
Cleanse your hearts and bring change
Amongst communities here and beyond.
The spread of new ideas is a phenomenon,
We can't stand against it in its entirety.
But change coming from strangers, most importantly,
Should be embraced cautiously.
This is the message for you and your progeny.
Of little significance, it may be now.
But not for our children
The message is for the coming generation.
Be kind, and ancestors shall bless your children.
Do good deeds, and when you depart,
A benediction shall come to your generation.
Wicked people produce evil spirits.
And therefore, evil ancestors,
Instilling negative energy to the community.
A benevolent soul becomes an ancestor.
And looks over his generation as an intercessor.
Serving as a direct link to the creator.
The performance of the remembrance ceremonial rites
A significant period to invite the ancestors within us.
When we place a request to our ancestors
During sacrifices, festivals, and rites
Who do you anticipate to reach?
When offering sacrifices,
Whose spirits do you invoke,
And chanted an incantation to?
Not the evil but benign ancestors.

The evil spirit is a nightmare
Devoid of positive inputs
Invades our dreams to create mayhem
And instill animosity within families.

Again, parents whose children serve them,
Diligently, don't usually depart the world
Without leaving behind everything they toiled.
That wish is for both parents and children.
However, that which a parent left for the children
Is ephemeral, no matter the amount of wealth accumulated
Should the parent end up
Not being benign ancestors.
It's not what we left on earth
That accomplishes the goal.
It's what the spirit of your ancestors
Send to us after departure.

At his prime age of twenty-five
Grown in endowment and virtue
His psychic about life remained incorruptible.
The power to meditate and heal
Became a spontaneous drill.
Hundreds of people came calling.
Certain he was an oracle of God's vocation.
Others claimed it was a family entitlement.
Because traditional healers had control
On such acts of palliating with their ancestors' approval.
Nevertheless, much to the surprise of villagers,
The beneficiary remained in denial.
Of the gift that hadn't come unanticipatedly.

Detractors peddled; he replicated acts of wizardry.
Similar to his deceased mother, accused of sorcery.

The propagation of his performance kingdom-wide
Brought to ambit the community consideration
Of Nnam being the new *Ndonge.*
Ndonge, in the Muane-Ngoe denotation
Means prophet, one whose presence
Denotes a traditional and cultural exhortation
Representing many things amongst its allure.
One ancestor had a mysterious assignation
And infused prophetic and healing prerogative
Within a defined and confined jurisdiction
In defense and protection of its people
And tribe during a crisis period and duration.
Or get a group of people caged,
From a preemptive enemy's altercation,
Any epidemic causing casualties of immense
Proportion, beyond human immediate extermination.
Before emerging, however, soothsayers would divine
Ndonge's assigned endeavors and apparition,
To perform as an intercessor during his tenure.

Was Nnam, therefore, the healer and prophet
Ancestors had promised would be the protector
Whose tribes and land were under occupation?
Perhaps he loved to practicalize his gift.
As an intermediary fit in the role of a facilitator.
After all, Elumpeh had prognosticated his reputation.
Even though at the time, he hadn't the explicit,
Knowledge to understand ancestral power

When interacting with its population
And in keeping with the almighty's commitment,
To anoint the people's endeavor,
Through the villagers' experience and anticipation.
Besides, it was no longer an argument.
That his power came from his ancestors.
But was the anointment for the defense and protection
Of the population rather than the healing
Of the people; committing atrocities,
Help reduce alarming sins,
Mend and restore broken hearts?
Again, embracing that responsibility
Involved the performance of rites
And the endorsement from villagers.
He believed to be an ordinary citizen.
Not called to embrace the Ndonge's qualification.
Because water action wasn't linked to his apparition
Which constituted one of the major distinctions
To qualify the Ndonge attribution.
He thus declined the Ndonge sort.
Believing to be the community's servant
Favored by the Ancestors and the Almighty.

The scars of the slave trade
Due to the licking peripheral sores
Still shockingly unbearable.
Like the 1772 Somersett's Habeas corpus,
The 1865 constitutional ratification and change
Of the triangular trade-system termination efforts
Were gaining grounds in the British Empire,
As in America; yet, these laws,

Weren't automatically applicable.
The continuation of the buoyant dead trade routes,
Persisted, as thousands remained captive
In the Ships and strange lands for decades,
Before colonization came hacking.
Fragmenting once more the vestiges,
Fostering the obliteration of the culture
And the traditional belief systems.
Dragging and lifting away, this time, not humans
But the endowment of their soil.
After both physical and mental
The devastation the people had undergone
For centuries, of no reason and fault of their own.

Who toils, produces abundant yields
Doesn't enjoy the fruits; he labors
And he's happy? The Muane-Ngoe man postulates.
This rhetoric question, when paralleled
In the context of Nnam's life,
Fit appropriately his newly embraced status
Having been subjected to torture
And starved most of his youthful life.
This seemed the time to bridge the cleave,
Between his pauper teenager life
And budding acquired prophetic healing fame,
That came with everything in abundance.

Expected to take pleasure in these delectables
Fate denied him for almost two decades.
Believers and followers from every domain
Those that had scorned and maltreated him,

Most of whom, he had healed to their incredulity.
And treated with kindness without any levy,
Visited and came with assorted gifts
And valuables to show their appreciation at intervals.
He ate none of it, neither did he use
The items in his healing practice.
Slaughtering and spilling of animal blood,
Didn't constitute part of his ritual performance.
Even though they received no condemnation.

The Bantu people like its Muane-Ngoe domain
Consider marriage the Hallmark of social responsibility
A man was incomplete without a woman
And children thereafter as in all cultural history.
Fit in the attributes of an admirable man
Tall, muscular, handsome and soft-spoken ebony.
And despite his newly attained position,
However, towards marriage, Nnam developed apathy.
And dotage Elumpeh refused to sanction that stand.
Calling him out of the necessity
As a man, and one with a clouded background,
And no parental guidance and family propinquity,
To temporarily fulfill that obligation.

Nnam's vocation to serve as a healer
Combining traditional medicine and theology
Didn't seem to be influenced by chance.
Ancestors and the Almighty had purposefully,
From infancy favored and redirected his course.
Accepting the call anyway,
Came with the unassailable challenge

From the environment of his emergence, primarily.

Before colonization and beyond, as with every healer,
Past theologians and traditional doctors,
The physical environment always had a profound
Effect on the practice of their calling and vocation.
The belief that God was in the skies of heaven,
And Mountains were a place to get closer to heaven,
Was as preponderance to the Hebrew
As it was to the Bantus people centuries before slavery.
Mountains were symbols of closeness to the Almighty.
And the Muane-Ngoe descendants experienced God and
their ancestors,
With the Muanenguba and Kupe Mountains.
At the time, predominantly active volcanoes.
To communion with the ancestral spirits
Through the performance of sacrifices and rites,
For long life, protection, prosperity
Good health and fertility and fecundity.

Full of sacred waters, the Muane-Ngoe landmass
Is characterized by tangible topography
With a cultural and traditional significance
Sanctified through mythology and history
Like the sacred waters in the bible
Exploited for cleansing, healing, initiation, and ceremony
Water, unending obsession for the people
Occurred across many Bantu ancestry
And is a central element in the pedigree
Of all Bantu cultures with mythology.

Featured in the Muane-Ngoe cultural groups
Life arises from this fundamental element.
The Noah's Ark account stands parallel
Ngoe's household flood myth.
A spirit in human form called Ngo-Nkang
Meaning a woman infested with dreadful scabies
Walked to each community and household
Soliciting for assistance, which no family
And person agreed to offer, scared,
Of her infested repellent body.
Upon arriving at Ngoe's hut, his wife
Moved by the visitor's agony
Compassion gripping her soul, she led her in.
Ngo-Nkang hadn't sat down,
When Ngoe stepped in and was hit
By a nauseating odor, he stepped back, quickly.
His wife immediately rushed out.
And provided an emphatic sympathetic entreaty.
Ngoe and wife provided her with shelter and food.
Ngo-Nkang, satisfied with their hospitality,
In the dead of night woke her hosts from sleep.
"Don't panic and listen carefully, she said.
I have walked through this community
And many others, far and beyond
In search of people with kind and generous hearts.
In my deplorable state, even water the Almighty
Has offered for free no one agreed to give me.
They all have treated me like a plague.
Someone not worthy of life.
But you showed me benevolence.
You showed me a sick and helpless person,

Has a place in your heart and house.
You demonstrated to me you deserve ancestral blessings.
For all that I have witnessed during these tribulations.
There shall occur a stormy and flash flood.
That will affect every living creature.
Within nine days, take your family
And everything you value
To the Cave by the mountainside.
Ngoe and wife went back to sleep.
But never saw Ngo-Nkang, again.
When it was the ninth day,
She mysteriously closed the cave.
The flood lasted for several weeks,
Ravaged every living thing it contacted.
By the time life returned to normal,
New physical features have developed.
Most importantly, the male and female twin lakes.
Representing Ngoe and his wife, Sumediang.
From that period, they experience unimaginable prosperity.

Sacred substances like in the bible
Influencing the categorizations of some waters.
And best integrated into rituals
As Christianity and Islam Faiths
That incorporate ritual washing
That occurred on the shores of Lake Galilee.
The Muanenguba twin lakes
Remain the spiritual force of the Muane-Ngoe people.
Known to serve as the underworld medium
Facilitating the science of necromancers.
Waterfalls, cataracts, river confluences, and catchments

Constituted sources of ritual performance and miracle
encounters.
Armed with this traditional and spiritual knowledge,
Nnam made periodic visits to the closest locations.
And yearly voyages to these distant complex topographies.
In keeping with traditional norms
And based on spiritual directives,
To attain certain objectives,
With complex challenges he encountered
To overcome problems and illnesses.

Secondarily, from contemporary healers and
Leaders of the communities, he emerged.
Nnam faced both mystical and physical raids,
To get into the core of his spiritual attainments.
Much of it geared towards discrediting his services.
Attempts at destroying the powers
And wanting to get him out of the scene,
For outperforming them in every measure
Because he exposed the charlatans.
And had an unmatched community following.

Nnam's infectious popularity remained a puller
Attracting faraway communities and healers
The leaders of the new order
Took notice and began sourcing for ways

To change his reflection on cultural beliefs.
That their ancestors had answers to all questions
Because they were the umbilical cord
Between mankind and God.

When duty called, once a mouth
Any of those secluded sites
Became a refuge for Nnam to stay far away
From the daily distraction and mounting pressure
To channel defined goals to his ancestors.
When he felt challenged in his faith
And had an impending task,
That needed more than the use of herbs to accomplish.
He went to secluded spots difficult to be reached,
Even by his patients and brethren to meditate.

It was the eleventh month,
It hadn't rained nor shine, colder or hotter,
To reflect the season, Nnam sat,
Meters away in the woods by the Nndum cataract.
A gentle breeze pushed his head, slower,
On to a mangrove tree to rest.
His soul and spirit instanter
Began to panegyrize to the most exalted.

Beyond and below, furthermost
Out of the human sphere
Nnam saddled between a rift valley
And dyad highlands with an irregular facet,
Of several volcanic spires
Burst and unburst projectiles and cavity.
A ridge cone-shape south to the dent
With steep sides having a step-form structure
Of many minor peaks locked in the lonely
Basement, of composite knolls shooting out
With savanna vegetation at the ridge.

A puffed lava sound flurry
From the epicenter surrounding the summit,
Similar to an earthquake.
A mass of fog towed out of the crater, majestically.
As the hypocenter produced a bubbling boiling tumult.
Installing a somber and terrifying atmosphere.

The grim and mystifying aura cast a spell.
A whispering of intoned indistinctive hex
Blowing toward Nnam, enforcing advection of fog,
Which formed a colossal yet magnificent pillar.
And frost dropping incessantly around the pillar.
Wearisome to depict before him the figure,
Nnam starred in bewilderment at the creature.
Vacillated into varying human forms and images
Completely out of place to suggest age.
He looked youthful and old at the same time,
Depending on the observer angle
Of elevation and inclination to visualize.
From the clouded picture appeared a bright face.
Sparkling like something smeared with diamond
Barefooted and half-naked,
Holding two bright, multicolor dowels and
Spreading his hands, written on his forehead;
'Alonge' life.
Gradually, Nnam feet left the soil.
As he rose to an angle of depression
Gazing at the mysterious figure, he quivered.
In disbelieve and maintaining the same speed,
He dropped at his initial position and prostrated,
In reverence and alarm.

If he was right, he thought before him,
Was standing a spirit of ancient times,
Of all ages, now, today, and the future.
In a slow audible but grumbling voice
Nnam heard the following hex;
"Behold, you are standing on sacred ground.
The cradle of the Bantu pedigree and command
The birth and return site
Where you came from during birth
And where you return after death.
One is born from the spirit,
At an appointed time, returns to the spirit.
No one returns where he hadn't originated.
No matter an individual's place of birth
And the subsequent place of death.
Everyone returns to his forebears.
Everyone you knew in your existence
Whose ancestors are of your bloodline
Or whose race and pedigree you share
Are nowhere else but here."

The voice dwindled gradually
The creature folding into a mass
As it came from the hypocenter.
Nnam raised his face and unexpectedly
Heard roaring trumpet sounds
Emanating northward, he fidgeted, and made a semi-cycle.
Staring upward, the creature cut through the topography,
Of volcanic high relief separated by countless rifts
With a broad-based savanna dominated, mostly
And two calderas relic mounts of tuff.

It flashed a sparkling flame and held a staff,
With the mane of a lion, adorned with gold.
The hair braided and dropping to the shoulders,
Covered with cowries and assorted beats.
The brawny torso, having the makings,
Of a woman, and on the forehead written;
Ndob (soil or earth)
A feeling of relief overcame the fright.
Approaching, Nnam began to feel the warmth.
He bowed, imagining the earth and life,
As a combination, the product was nothing else,
But man, the cradle and finality of the Bantu people.
If there was anything else to discern
About humanity, he seemed standing where it began,
The genesis of the Bantu creation.
If not, then perhaps, he was at the continuance,
Of the route that led straight to the birthplace,
Of man's creation and nature.
The origin of fables and allegories of poverty,
That of riches, evil and benevolence, fertility and sterility.

"Behold, you gladden your ancestor's heart.
Inspired to do good and safeguard your descent
From pursuing the evil path
That has made uninhabitable many communities
As established for humanity to partake
In its ancestral endowment.
Steadfast in faith
Cast off the devil's wiles
Having swallowed the pains
And wrestled against the trappings of the flesh.

Taken away from the darkness of the earth
You withstood darkened spirited forces
Demonstrating the danger of wickedness.
A great light has shown on your worthiness
From your ancestors' favor flows
Ushering you into the creators' territory
Making you a partaker of divine force.
A new creature leveled above human life
Equipped to be welcomed by your ancestors
In preparation for a place with the creator
Where no room exists for the ephemeral pleasure.
But eternally in abundance for they that heed to the voice.

A sudden surge of light
Rushed through his corpse
And put away the sulfur of human sins.
Completing the cleansing of the remains
Of anything that seemed linked with humans.
"Here you are now clothed with a garment.
The ancestral garment that shells out
Worldly activities and purify
To usher in greater love and peace.

The earth and life made a cuddling symmetry.
And gradually, they pulled apart parallelly,
As Nnam watched, stupefied.
Between them appeared hybrid colorless,
But magnificent inscriptions in bold words.
And Alonge enunciated them to him:
"The gate of life
The mysteries gate

Seven gates
Seven tribes"
Every gate with an entrance
That led to the mystery's gate
That led to the gate of life.
Engulfed by the spirit of eagerness
He could perceive nothing else
Except for an endless amount of attainable desires.
In the glory of his deeds and services.

At the augury, leadership and exhortation
Of Ndob, they walked by the middle gate.
Nnam remained between them.
And behold, a flash of glorious light,
Shown so unexpectedly bright
Like a mask pulled off Nnam's face
And scales falling from his eyes,
Brightening his vision and perception.
The light brought to ambit a landmass,
So endlessly spacious and fathomless.
Yet he could see its multiple constituents.
His eyes hovered the clouds.
Capturing the precincts set for the unfolding
Of centuries lost and searched for answers.
An eyesore of evil vile and human waste,
Of an unfathomable proposition, took over.
Before being overwhelmed with a myriad
Of most beautiful features never seen before
And couldn't retain much of what came
From the sphere, except the growing desire
And the wish of stepping passed the gate.

"Beyond these gates is the journeys' end.
There's no returning to the earth, alive.
Out of these gates to earth
The only possible return is a new creation.
A return with a rejuvenated soul.
Past attributes may follow the pristine creation.
In an elevated, and much improved,
Or a degenerated form of human.

Nnam's exploratory wish came to a halt
But not the ability to seek for answers.
"Can you show me the devil?"
"The devil, you say?" He replied; Nnam nodded.
"Look right, he continued, and behind.
And in front, whom did you see?"
Hesitantly, "I saw no one."
"There's no such separately made creature
In both human and supernatural spheres
Send to mankind as the Devil.
In every living being's mind is stalled evil.
The urge to do wrong or right
Live concomitantly in the mind.
Anything evil is human creation
And it comes in no defined form,
From both living and death spirits

Nnam woke from the spiritual journey, dazed
Seeing himself in an aura so leaden
About a hundred meters within the surrounding fringes.
Wondering, did he bore witness of a double apparition,
Or was he hallucinating in the darkness of the woods?

A gentle breeze from the cataracts' direction
Filled his sweating pores.
Reached for his staff spear and with vigor stood.
Chanting indistinctive hexes
Stretched his muscular hands
Pinned the spear on the ground
And hopped around it seven times.
Overtaken by the mysteries of his revelation,
From that day on, he made routine visitation
Within the Nndum cataract area with a preoccupation
Of bringing to reality his vision.

If Nnam medicinal ability
Was anything before the divine encounter
He became an unchallenged authority.
If he was a rising traditional preacher
At the inception, his level of sanctity,
Became incomparable to any known theologian
Kingdom-wide and beyond. However, shorty
His preoccupation shifted to something tougher
And complex, new and strange to the community.
Producing two physical representations of his encounter.
The source of his healing proficiency,
Pulling him away from his assigned endeavors.

Nnam had no formal pottery knowledge.
Neither did he in iron smelting
In sculpting, he had a smattering ability.
He wished he took advantage
When he was homeless and spent months living
With a man who geared his youthful viability

In the mastering of the craft of sculpture.
These skills notability were prevailing,
Around and within the Muane-Ngoe territory.
Even though few individuals patronize craftsmanship
And the Ngeme-Ngoe kingdom,
Hadn't produced anyone the likes of Nzitone
Who joined the ancestors almost a century,
With countless others, the results of slavery.

With limited knowledge to attain his objectives
Combined with the complexity of the attributes
Of the personalities, he intended to portray
Getting assistance from a single source
The results, he was convinced, would be unsatisfactory.
Nnam employed the services of three men and one woman.
Nsong the sculpture
Ehabweh the iron smelter,
Nkumbe, a specialist in general craftsmanship
And Njepolle the potter.
These artisans from the inception of his enlistment;
As an oracle of the ancestors,
Had followed Nnam diligently.
Without narrating his experience to this crew,
He asked Nkumbe to produce a sketch,
By giving an eye-catching description.
Combining hard work and imagination,
Nnam and his team spent six months,
To erect the statue of Ndob and Alonge.

CPSIA information can be obtained
at www.ICGtesting.com
Printed in the USA
BVHW051517210323
660848BV00015B/691